THE OTTAWA

ELAINE LANDAU

THE OTTAWA

Franklin Watts   A Division of Grolier Publishing
New York   London   Hong Kong   Sydney   Danbury, Connecticut
A First Book

Map by Joe LeMonnier
Cover photograph copyright ©: Ben Klaffke
Photographs copyright ©: Ben Klaffke: pp. 3, 8, 14. 18 (both), 23, 25, 31 (both),
33, 34, 38, 50, 55, 56; National Archives of Canada: pp. 20, 28, 46 (Joshua Jebb);
Carnegie Library of Pittsburgh: p. 40; The Library of Congress: p. 44.

Library of Congress Cataloging-in-Publication Data

The Ottawa / by Elaine Landau.
 p. cm. — (A First book)
Includes bibliographical references and index.
Summary: Describes the life of the Indians who established villages in the area of
Lake Huron where there were forests, rivers, and favorable conditions for growing
crops.
ISBN 0-531-20226-7 (hrd cover)   ISBN 0-531-15783-0 (trd pbk)
1. Ottawa Indians — Juvenile literature. [1. Ottawa Indians. 2. Indians of North
America.] I. Title. II. Series.
E99.O9L34 1996
977'.004973—dc20   95-49036 CIP AC

CONTENTS

For Michael Pearl

SUNRISE IN OTTAWA COUNTRY: THE OTTAWA
OFTEN BUILT THEIR VILLAGES NEAR WATERWAYS.

THE OTTAWA

Winter was nearly over, and the Indians of a small village in what is now Michigan eagerly awaited spring. During the bitter-cold months, they had worked outdoors hunting and trapping animals. This was essential to their survival but not just because the animals were an important food source for them.

These Indians were also especially interested in fur pelts. *Bartering* with the French traders who had recently arrived in North America, they exchanged fur pelts for guns, ammunition, axes, iron cooking pots, knives, prespun cloth, and trinkets. They also served as middlemen in the fur trade between the French and other Indian tribes to the northwest in what is today Montreal, Quebec. They were the Ottawa—a people whose name comes from the word *adawe*, which in their language means "to trade."

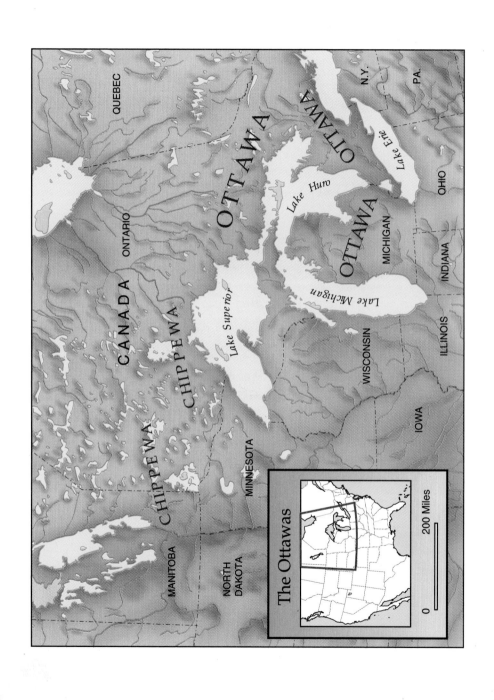

The Ottawas

0   200 Miles

Throughout their history, the Ottawa often moved to new areas for a variety of reasons. At different times these Americans Indians inhabited various coastal regions of what is now the Michigan Lower Peninsula, nearby portions of Ontario, Canada, and parts of Ohio, Indiana, and Wisconsin. Later on, some Ottawa were relocated to Kansas and eventually Oklahoma.

But when they first came in contact with Europeans, the Ottawa mainly lived in villages in three Lake Huron locations presently known as Manitoulin Island, the Bruce Peninsula, and the north and east shores of Georgian Bay. These regions tended to be heavily forested with a mixture of hardwood and conifer (evergreen, cone-bearing) trees. The rivers contained an abundant variety of fish as well as both game and *waterfowl*. The temperate climate, good soil conditions, and adequate rainfall further made it an ideal area for growing crops and establishing villages. This is where the Ottawa settled and it's where our story of their lives begins.

THE FOUR SEASONS: AN OTTAWA YEAR

The Ottawa's daily activities varied with the seasons. During the summer, the women tended the crops while the men repaired the canoes, weapons, tools, and houses. Although there was always work to do in the village, summer was also a time for special celebrations. Depending on the occasion, the feasting and dancing might last well into the night.

Lacrosse, a ball game in which two teams compete, was especially popular among the Ottawa. In the summer, Ottawa in neighboring villages often staged these competitions for everyone to enjoy. Small groups of Ottawa also played various games within their own villages using straws, animal bones, and dice. During the warmer months, games of chance and gambling were common among these American Indians as well.

The Ottawa, however, could not afford to be entirely off guard. Just as summer meant more time for village sports and festivities, it was also when disputes were settled and wrongs avenged through war. A young man's first experience as a member of an Ottawa war party was likely to take place during the summer. Similarly, during this time the Ottawa made sure enough men were always present in their villages to resist attacks from other tribes.

When fall arrived, Ottawa women busily harvested the crops planted earlier that year. Any extra vegetables, along with the additional berries picked over the summer, were dried and stored away in underground pits. Meanwhile the men hunted the waterfowl flying south for the winter. Whatever wasn't eaten was smoked (*smoking* is a way of treating meat or fish to preserve it) and put into storage. The same was done with the extra game hunted.

The Ottawa secured most of their food for the upcoming months by autumn's end. That's because their winters were largely spent hunting and trapping animals whose fur pelts could be traded to the French. Luxurious furs were highly sought after in

A BEAVER PELT STRETCHED ACROSS A FRAME:
SUCH PELTS WERE IN GREAT DEMAND
AMONG EUROPEAN TRADERS.

upper-class European circles. The wealthy wanted fur garments both for warmth and as a sign of prestige. Once European fur resources had been exhausted, they looked to those of North America to satisfy the demand.

Nearly all the Ottawa left the village for the winter hunt. Usually only the elderly, sick, and perhaps a few people to care for them stayed behind. The rest of the villagers set out in family hunting parties for areas where there was abundant game and adequate shelter in which to set up temporary housing. While in the woods, Ottawa men stalked bears and deer and laid traps for beavers, foxes, otters, and raccoons. How well the Indians did influenced the group's well-being for the upcoming year. A poor trapping season meant less to trade. And because they were trade middlemen, that could doubly hurt the Ottawa.

But if the hunters did well, they savored the rewards of their winter toil that spring. Traveling along the waterways in their birchbark canoes each spring, they stopped to trade with other tribes as well as at French forts and settlements. Although the French were mainly interested in furs, the Ottawa also traded cornmeal, sunflower oil, rugs or mats, tobacco, and healing roots and herbs for European goods.

Once the bartering was completed, the Ottawa returned to their villages. The women prepared the plots of land surrounding the village for spring planting. Starting in the spring and continuing through the summer, Ottawa males fished. Although they didn't spend as much time hunting as in the fall and winter, some of the men and boys went off on hunting trips. Gearing their lives to nature's seasonal changes, these accomplished traders survived the challenges of their environment.

FOOD, CLOTHING, AND TOOLS

Before their lives were forever altered by repeated contact with whites, the Ottawa largely met their own needs. They looked to the land, rivers, plants, and animals around them for their food, clothing, and tools.

Ottawa women farmed using sharp wooden digging sticks to break the ground. Wood, as well as stone, was also important to Ottawa men in making bows and arrows. Before guns became available, these were crucial for hunting and warfare. Wooden clubs and spears, and wood and stone *tomahawks* made by the Ottawa were useful for these purposes as well.

Birchbark canoes constructed from the bark and wood of the area's trees were essential to the tribe's well-being. These lightweight, durable boats allowed

THE OTTAWA LIVED OFF THE LAND'S BOUNTY.
THE MEN FISHED BOTH ALONE AND IN GROUPS,
AND THE WOMEN PLANTED CORN.

Ottawa traders to travel speedily along the region's waterways to their various destinations. Canoe travel also permitted the Ottawa to reach broader hunting and fishing areas when necessary. Ottawa men hunted and fished in groups as well as by themselves. In good times, they would return to their camps with an abundant variety of meat and fish.

It was up to the women to clean and cook the fish and animals. A fresh kill or catch could be prepared in a variety of ways. Depending on what was available, the food might be fried, roasted, or boiled. At times portions of the meat or fish were made in a hearty soup.

The Ottawa also heavily relied on *pemmican*—a food made by pounding dried meat into a powder and mixing it with bear fat and berries. Pemmican was an excellent source of nutrition for the winter. There was no spoilage, and it could be easily transported or eaten while traveling.

In the spring, Ottawa women tapped the area's maple trees for sap. They would slash the tree and insert a wooden spout in the hole for the thick fluid to flow out of. The sap was collected in birchbark pails placed beneath the spouts. After they had eaten mostly meat and dried food all winter, the sweet-tasting syrup tasted especially delicious.

AS SHOWN HERE, MANY OTTAWA MEN
HAD BODY TATTOOS.

The women also extended their food supply by planting peas, beans, squash, pumpkins, and other crops. These vegetables might be eaten fresh, ground into meal, or baked into bread. They also gathered an assortment of wild edible fruits, nuts, and plants.

Before the introduction of prespun cloth from Europe, Ottawa women made their family's clothing from available materials in their environment. Early Ottawa clothing, however, was not very elaborate. In the warmer months, the Ottawa often wore little more than a *breechclout*—a deerskin covering placed around the hips and thighs. When it became colder, fur cloaks and *moccasins* were added.

Although they dressed simply, Ottawa males adorned their bodies in other ways. They wore copper, stone, and shell ornaments in their pierced ears and noses. Some wore feathers around their necks and in their ears. Ottawa men also frequently placed feathers in their hair, which they wore short and upright in front. Body *tattoos* and face painting were also common among them.

OTTAWA VILLAGES AND GOVERNMENT

The Ottawa often built their villages near bodies of water. This provided easy access to the water they needed for daily living as well as a means to reach other tribes by canoe when trading.

An average Ottawa village contained about thirty "longhouses." These structures were one-and-a-half stories high and sometimes extended 130 feet (40 m) in length. Ottawa longhouses were made of long poles secured in the ground that curved to close at the top. Within each of the houses, three or four fires blazed with two to three families sharing a fire. In some areas, the Ottawa built fortlike stockades around their villages as protection from enemy raiding parties. Just beyond their villages were their small farming plots.

WHILE AT THEIR HUNTING SITES, THE
OTTAWA LIVED IN SMALL TEMPORARY
CIRCULAR HOUSES SUCH AS THIS ONE.

The Ottawa's permanent village homes differed from the temporary dwellings they used while on the move. These smaller structures housed one or two families and largely consisted of a circle of poles overlapping at the top to form a sort of dome. This framework was covered with birchbark strips and mats woven from reeds. When the Indians were ready to leave a particular hunting site, the women dismantled the structure. The poles might be left there for use the following year, while the mats were rolled up and taken along to their next destination.

Ottawa villages were not governed by a strict code of regulations. Because the Ottawa lived in such close quarters, there was simply a good deal of family and community pressure to behave properly. Each village had a council of elders that dealt with questions and issues concerning the village's general well-being and future. The council elders tended to be older Ottawa men who had demonstrated both wisdom and patience in their dealings with others.

Each Ottawa village also had one or more civil chiefs. These men represented and spoke for the council of elders within the village, with other Ottawa groups, and with neighboring American Indian tribes. Civil chiefs tended to be highly respected in their communities and could usually persuade others to

A MODEL OF THE INSIDE OF
AN OTTAWA DWELLING

accept their way of thinking. Unlike succession within European royal families, the position of civil chief was generally not passed from father to son. While coming from a powerful and influential Ottawa family might help someone become a civil chief, any Ottawa male with strong leadership qualities could hold this post.

In addition to its civil chief, each Ottawa village had a separate war chief. A war chief led his men in conflicts with other Indian tribes and later on in the Ottawa's struggle against the whites. Ottawa war chiefs were usually chosen because of their outstanding battle feats. A war chief was expected to both develop winning war strategies and inspire his men to follow him.

Being an Ottawa village leader held a good deal of promise. A well-known, especially distinguished civil or war chief might eventually be asked to represent several of the area's villages. On the other hand, an ineffective chief or one who was guilty of misconduct could be asked to step down.

OTTAWA FAMILIES

Family bonds were important to the Ottawa, and living so near one another, these families tended to be close. While divorce was possible, it was frowned upon, especially if the couple had children. In these cases, usually both the husband's and wife's families would try to persuade the couple to stay together.

The birth of a child was an important family event. This was especially so if the baby was a boy. Several months after the infant was born there would be a special tribal ceremony at which the child was given a name. Not just any name would do. It had to be a name used by the child's family in the past—one that was a meaningful part of the young person's heritage. Sometimes the infant's ears and nose were also pierced at the ceremony. Tiny ornaments inserted in these openings were believed to shield the baby from

AN OTTAWA MAN, WOMAN, AND CHILD: CHILDREN WERE AN IMPORTANT PART OF OTTAWA FAMILY LIFE.

evil and harm. The baby's parents also gave a feast for this special occasion.

Ottawa children usually spent their first few years of life on a cradleboard covered with goose down. Sometimes their mothers carried these cradleboards on their backs so they could care for the children as they completed their daily tasks. In the house, cradleboards were often propped up against the wall, so the children could see and hear what was going on around them.

The Ottawa did not rely on strict rules or severe punishments in raising their children. Young Ottawa learned early on that at certain times it was crucial to be completely silent. Any human sound—crying or laughing out loud—could be disastrous if they were hiding from an enemy.

As Ottawa children grew older, they were schooled in the ways of their people. Young boys were taught to use bows and arrows for hunting and war. Sometimes the most important lessons took the form of play. Male children practiced valuable hunting, fishing, and fighting techniques through games and exercises geared to developing these skills. Once the Ottawa assumed their role as trade middlemen with the Europeans, boys were taught to trade as well as to use the new items introduced by the whites. This meant learning how to best employ European hunting traps, fishing nets, and steel axes. As guns began to replace bows and arrows, Ottawa youths practiced marksmanship.

Among other tasks, Ottawa girls were taught to gather and prepare food, grow crops, *tan* animal hides, set up temporary shelters, and make clothes for their families. Their daily lives and chores were also changed through increased trade with whites. Prespun cloth from Europe largely replaced the animal skins the women had always used for clothing. Iron cooking kettles and containers were also often used instead of the clay pots and baskets made by Ottawa women.

When the youths grew older, they would choose a mate. Ottawa marriages were not prearranged by parents or the village elders. Instead young people were generally allowed to marry whomever they wished. Usually it was someone from their village or a nearby Ottawa village. Once a young couple agreed to marry, the young man presented his future in-laws with several valuable gifts in return for their daughter.

Although Ottawa men were allowed to have more than one wife, this was fairly uncommon. A man with two or three families was expected to support them all. And when game was scarce, providing for even a single family could be difficult.

OTTAWA WOMEN WERE SKILLED BASKET MAKERS. THEY
COLLECTED NATURAL MATERIALS FROM THEIR SURROUNDINGS
(ABOVE) TO WEAVE VINE BASKETS (BELOW).

RELIGION

Numerous Ottawa legends reflect these American Indians' beliefs about the world and their place in it. According to one ancient tale, the tribe descended from three families. One of these families was that of Michabou, a tremendously strong and powerful fisherman known as The Great Hare. The Ottawa credited Michabou with many awe-inspiring feats. Besides forming the earth it was said that he could stand and fish in more than 100 feet (30 m) of water, and the water level would still only reach his armpits. Michabou was also thought to have invented fishnets to enable the Ottawa to catch more fish. Supposedly the idea came to him after he watched a spider capture its prey in its netlike web.

HERE OTTAWA YOUTHS HELP PREPARE A CEREMONIAL FIRE.
NUMEROUS AMERICAN INDIAN RITES AND CEREMONIES
HAVE BEEN PASSED DOWN THROUGH THE AGES.

THE OTTAWA USED MEDICINE WHEELS SUCH AS THE
ONE SHOWN HERE. IF HUNG NEAR AN ILL PERSON,
THEY BELIEVED IT WOULD CATCH THE EVIL SPIRITS
HARMING THE INDIVIDUAL.

The ancient tale holds that another of the Ottawa families descended from a fish known as the Namepich, or Carp. According to the legend, one day after *spawning*, this fish left its eggs on the shores of a riverbank. But when the eggs hatched there were no fish to be found. Instead a beautiful woman appeared. This woman's children are thought to have been the start of a second Ottawa family.

The third family was that of the Bearpaw. There is no legend to explain how this group began. Yet as late as the eighteenth century, Ottawa who believed they descended from the Bearpaw family performed special rites to honor the bear. Whenever a bear was killed, they would give a celebration. The festivities included a lavish feast at which they spoke highly of the bear and ate its meat, believing it would give them the animal's shrewdness and bravery.

The Ottawa also believed that their lives were affected by a number of both benevolent and evil spirits. These included an all-powerful supreme being known as *Kicci-manito*, or the "Master of Life." On various occasions the Ottawa made offerings of tobacco, corn, or other foods to the benevolent beings to win their favor. Offerings were also sometimes made to avoid their anger.

Some Ottawa men and women became members of a select group known as the Mitewiwin, or Medicine Society. These individuals were called upon to cure the sick. Besides relying on medicinal plants and herbs, they appealed to the spirits for help in healing the person.

Sometimes the ill individuals recovered; other times they died. But either way the Ottawa accepted their fate. They believed that everyone has two souls—only one of which dies with the person's body. The person's other soul was thought to undertake a perilous journey to the next world. Once it arrived at its final destination, however, the dead person's spirit spent eternity in a safe and beautiful land.

Although the French Jesuit missionaries tried to convert the Ottawa to Christianity, they were largely unsuccessful. As a free and unconquered people, these American Indians clung fiercely to their beliefs.

THE WHITES' ASSAULT

Although the Ottawa and other Indian tribes thrived in North America for centuries, the large numbers of oncoming whites eventually threatened their existence. Rivalry between England and France for North American dominance heightened over time. And as the two powers competed for the continent's resources, American Indian groups tended to side with one or the other.

The Ottawa had enjoyed a long and close relationship with France. In trading with the French, they had always been dealt with fairly. Although the Ottawa did not readily convert to Christianity, French *missionaries* had also treated them well. The Ottawa's

A SIDE VIEW OF AN OTTAWA AREA MISSION HOUSE: FRENCH MISSIONARIES SENT TO NORTH AMERICA BEFRIENDED THE OTTAWA AND OTHER AMERICAN INDIAN GROUPS.

ties to France were further strengthened when their enemies, the Iroquois, allied themselves with the British.

Unfortunately the Ottawa were among the Indian groups that became deeply embroiled in the ongoing North American struggle between England and France. The French and Indian Wars, as they were called, consisted of a series of conflicts waged between 1689 and 1763. While the hostilities were primarily between the two European powers, a number of Indian nations fought on both sides and were often a pivotal force in winning battles.

Among the Indians who distinguished themselves in the fighting was the Ottawa war chief Pontiac. The son of a war chief himself, Pontiac seemed destined for greatness even as a young boy growing up in his Ottawa village. By the time he was thirty he was well known on both sides of the Atlantic as a courageous fighter, an able leader, and a brilliant battle planner.

On numerous occasions during the French and Indian Wars, Pontiac swayed the balance of power in France's favor. This was particularly evident in 1755 when the British sent an especially large number of troops to North America under the direction of General William Braddock. Attempting to capture a

CHIEF PONTIAC INSPIRED HIS OWN PEOPLE
AS WELL AS OTHER AMERICAN INDIANS TO REBEL
AGAINST THE EUROPEAN TYRANNY.

fort in what is now Pittsburgh, Braddock had his soldiers march through the forest toward their destination. Beating their drums while dressed in the bright-red coats of their uniforms, the marching soldiers were easy to spot.

Pontiac took full advantage of this military blunder by ambushing the British in the woods. The Indians, accompanied by a few Frenchmen, hid behind trees remaining close to the ground as they fired on the enemy. The confused British troops fired back but were unable to hit a target they couldn't see. General Braddock was killed while many other British soldiers either died or were wounded. This was just one of the times in which Pontiac, along with his Indian allies, was invaluable to the French.

Despite their assistance, France was eventually defeated. This left the Indians who had been loyal to the French in a difficult position. They lost their trade connection to Europe along with the other advantages of their friendship with the French.

The Ottawa's future looked especially bleak because their enemies the Iroquois had always traded with the British as well as fought on the winning side. But perhaps most devastating to the Ottawa was their treatment by the British after the French were expelled.

Unlike the French, the British felt the Indians were racially inferior to them and exploited the Ottawa and other tribes in countless ways. British fur traders continually cheated them, and settlers and businessmen were eager to seize the Indians' lands.

Government policy towards American Indians was equally disgraceful. After Britain's North American victory, Lord Jeffrey Amhurst was sent to command British military forces in the New World. Amhurst was a bigot who favored using any means to be rid of the Indians. Hoping to wipe them out, he suggested that blankets used by white smallpox patients be sent to the Indians as a false gesture of friendship. Unfortunately, *smallpox* and other diseases the Indians contracted from whites took a severe toll on their strength and numbers.

Amhurst's monetary policies toward the American Indians were equally severe. He reduced funding by more than 40 percent for the Indian Department that had been set up to help American Indians. He also stopped the practice of presenting the Indians with gifts of much needed supplies for the upcoming winter. The French had done this for years as a token of their goodwill. Such measures caused a great deal of concern among the Ottawa as well as other Indian tribes west of the Appalachian Mountains. They knew that if they didn't take action they'd be trampled on by the whites.

The Indians emotions were also fueled by a American Indian religious leader known as "The Prophet." The Prophet preached that Native Americans needed to believe in themselves and push back the whites. He felt that if the Indians returned to their ancient ways, they would throw off their oppressors and continue as a people.

Feeling defeated and deceived by the whites, many of the area Indian groups heeded The Prophet's words. Representatives from a number of midwestern tribes met to plan a united uprising against the British. Once again the Ottawa war chief Pontiac rose to a prominent position. He led the Ottawa—along with several other tribes, including the Chippewa, Miami, and Peoria—against the British.

In May 1763, Pontiac and his men launched an attack on a British fort in what is now Detroit. Although the British suffered serious losses, they managed to hold the heavily stockaded fort. But Pontiac, whose village was just miles away, refused to retreat. Instead, he kept Fort Detroit under siege for

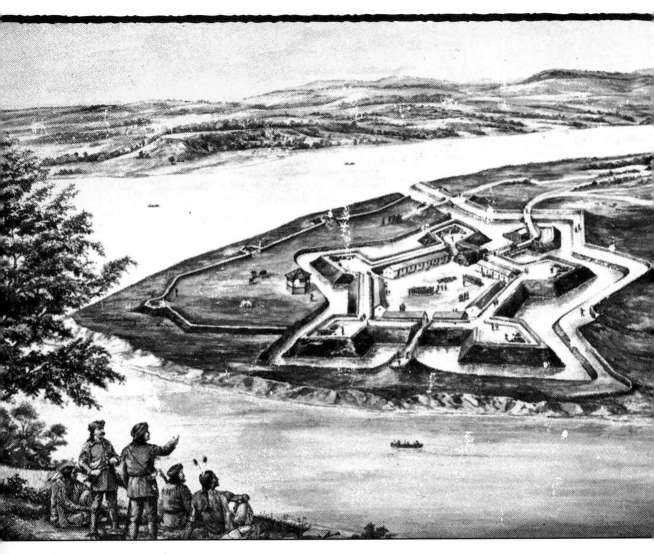

FORT PITT (SHOWN HERE) WAS AMONG THE
BRITISH POSTS BESIEGED BY PONTIAC'S
ALLIED INDIAN FORCES.

more than two months, relentlessly firing on the British whenever he had the chance. At the same time Pontiac's men also raided white settlements in the surrounding countryside.

Pontiac's Detroit assault inspired other tribes to do the same. Within weeks Indians attacked a number of forts, often causing them to fall. By the end of July, only three British forts in the west were left intact, and these remained under siege by the Indians.

Nevertheless, lacking the weaponry and other resources to bring down Fort Detroit, Pontiac knew he eventually would have to concede. This became especially apparent after the British sent in supplies and troop reinforcements. Pontiac began to lose faith in The Prophet's vision and the hope that the French would return to assist in his efforts. Reluctantly he agreed to a truce with the British.

The truce permitted Pontiac to move his people to what is presently Illinois. He hoped they would recover there and perhaps launch another offensive against the British. But although his own people still followed him, support from neighboring tribes began to falter. Some who had been badly beaten by the British felt unable to continue. By 1764, many of Pontiac's Indian allies had given up the notion of another uprising, and in that year they attended British peace conferences.

HERE TWO OTTAWA CHIEFS FROM THE LAKE HURON AREA
PREPARE TO MEET WITH BRITISH OFFICIALS.

Despite the apparent lack of Indian forces available to Pontiac, the British were still concerned about future attacks from him. To head off further trouble, they sent a group of delegates to work out a lasting peace with him. Seeing few available alternatives, Pontiac agreed to a peace *treaty* with the British in October 1765, ending the uprising known as "Pontiac's Rebellion." Pontiac was later approached by the French to join them in an attempt to regain the territory they had lost to the British. Having agreed to the terms of the peace treaty, however, he refused to go back on his word.

RELOCATION

While the Ottawa already lived in a number of locations, the stream of white settlers from the East eventually scattered them even further. Outnumbered and outgunned, Ottawa and other American Indians were forced to agree to treaties depriving them of the lands that they had hunted and fished on for years. Their plight worsened when in many instances the U.S. government failed to live up to its treaties once the Indians' territory had been seized.

One government-ordered Indian relocation occurred in the 1830s when the Ottawa, along with several other Indian tribes living in what is now Ohio, were taken to the area presently known as Kansas.

Although some Ottawa hid out in Ohio and others fled to Canada, the government moved most of them to Kansas in a series of three trips.

For the most part the transports proceeded smoothly. Yet at times some ugly incidents occurred. One such incident took place after an elderly Ottawa chief refused to sign the treaty agreeing to the relocation. Needing his signature, a small group of white men posing as friends got him drunk and guided his hand as the chief signed the document without knowing what he was doing. Once he was sober and realized what had happened, he claimed the document wasn't valid and refused to join the transport.

But the chief's protests were ignored. Soldiers bound his hands and feet and threw him into a wagon heading west. He wasn't untied until they arrived in Kansas. By then he was too sick and exhausted to protest further. He never adjusted to his new surroundings and died several months later.

The Indians' Kansas *reservation* (the land given them by the government) consisted of 74,000 acres (almost 30,000 ha) on which the various Ottawa families were allotted homesteads. Surprisingly, the new land proved to be quite desirable. There were heavily wooded areas filled with game as well as rivers and streams containing a variety of fish. But unfortunately

TO SURVIVE, AMERICAN INDIANS HAVE OFTEN HAD TO
ADAPT TO THE WHITE WORLD. THIS IS EVIDENT
THROUGH THESE OTTAWA MUSICIAN'S CLOTHING
STYLES AND CHOICE OF INSTRUMENTS.

the appealing region also attracted white settlers, and in the 1860s portions of the reservation were sold off to white homesteaders by the government.

The money paid for the acreage was to be held in trust for the Indians. When Ottawa leaders inquired about the sum, however, they were told that the money had been misplaced and could not be accounted for. Clearly the Ottawa had once again been cheated out of what was rightfully theirs.

As time passed, increasing numbers of whites pressed government officials for homesteads on the Ottawa's land. The property was also thought to be ideal for the railroads expanding west through Kansas. Fearful that the government would sell their land and again "misplace" the money, the Ottawa decided to take action on their own.

John Wilson, the Ottawa's chief at the time, sought government approval to purchase land in "Indian Territory," an area set aside for various relocated Indian tribes in what is now Oklahoma. Wilson hoped that his people would be better off in this region because it was not as desirable to the whites. Therefore between 1869 and 1870 the majority of the Ottawa who came to Kansas from Ohio moved to a tract of land in Oklahoma.

It was a difficult journey for the Ottawa, who were still angry at the government and its Indian agent for the loss of their funds. Unfortunately quite a few of the Indians died, both during the trip and soon after arriving. They had not been the only Ottawa to lose their land because of the whites' greed and expansion. An 1836 treaty provided that large numbers of Michigan Ottawa be sent to live on Manitoulin Island. Yet despite the various relocations, the Ottawa continued as a people.

PAST AND PRESENT

In more recent times, groups of Ottawa have lived in Oklahoma, Michigan, Wisconsin, and parts of Ontario, Canada. Often they have faced serious obstacles to continuing their way of life. In some cases, these American Indians have been left hard pressed for funds while federal services to them were cut off. Through the years large numbers of Ottawa were forced to borrow money against their land allotments. Unable to repay these loans, they lost their property. The situation worsened when their hunting and fishing rights guaranteed by treaties were frequently ignored by local and state authorities.

Finding it increasingly difficult to live as they had in the past, the Ottawa adapted to the white world.

This was especially true for those in Oklahoma and the northern Lower Peninsula of Michigan, where there was a great deal of intermarriage between the Ottawa and whites as well as many Ottawa working in white industries. In time, the Ottawa's language was rarely heard in Oklahoma, just as most of the ancient traditions were no longer observed as they were by Ottawa in other areas.

Yet while many Ottawa have embraced white America's customs, they have still not forgotten who they are or where they came from. In recent years, a number of Oklahoma Ottawa have taken steps to revive their culture. They've held powwows where they have danced to their people's traditional music. Some have also shown a renewed interest in their people's legends and ancient beliefs.

Other Ottawa have enjoyed a cultural reawakening as well. Among them is Frank Ettawageshik, a Michigan Ottawa who makes pottery in the tradition and design of his ancestors. Fashioning these pots entirely by hand, he creates distinctive cord markings with thin strips of basswood bark. Ettawageshik's work has been displayed in numerous galleries and museums.

Like his father, a well-known Ottawa storyteller, Frank Ettawageshik has helped preserve his people's

OTTAWA POTTER FRANK ETTAWAGES~~~~~~ HERE)
HAS CONDUCTED INDIAN POTTERY W~~~~~PS WITH
LOCAL ELEMENTARY SCHOOL CHILDR~~~~~PS WITH
STUDENTS GATHERED AND PREPARED ~~~~~RIALS
FOR THE PROJECT BEFORE MAKING ~~~~~TS.

A SAMPLING OF FRANK ETTAWAGESHIK'S
POTTERY PIECES

ancient tales and legends by practicing this art as well. The stories he tells today have been passed down by Ottawa for generations.

Ettawageshik has also kept Ottawa culture alive by teaching his children traditional Ottawa pottery-making techniques. One of his sons even sold enough pieces to purchase a BMX bike. That's an example of how some Ottawa are combining present-day life with past traditions. The Ottawa have survived the challenges of the past and are likely to continue to survive those of the future.

GLOSSARY

Bartering trading

Breechclout a piece of animal skin worn around the hips and thighs

Kicci-manito, or the **"Master of Life"** an all-powerful supreme being the Ottawas believed in

Lacrosse a ball game played on a field in which two opposing teams use long-handled netted rackets to drive the ball

Missionary an individual who attempts to convert others to his or her religious beliefs

Moccasin a soft leather shoe worn by the Ottawas and other Indians

Pemmican an American Indian food made by pounding dried meat into a powder and mixing it with bear fat and berries

Reservation land set aside for the Indians by the government

Smallpox an extremely contagious viral disease characterized by a scarring rash

Smoking treating meat or fish by exposing it to smoke in order to preserve it

Spawning the laying of eggs by a fish

Tomahawk an axe formerly used by some Native Americans as a tool and weapon

Tanning a process through which an animal hide or skin is turned into leather

Tattoo an image or design permanently etched on a person's skin

Treaty an agreement between nations

Waterfowl a waterbird or swimming game bird

FOR FURTHER READING

Ancona, George. *Powwow*. San Diego: Harcourt, 1993.

Avery, Susan and Linda Skinner. *Extraordinary American Indians*. Chicago: Children's Press, 1992.

Blakely, Martha. *Native Americans and the U.S. Government*. New York: Chelsea House, 1995.

Bland, Celia. *Pontiac: Ottawa Rebel*. New York: Chelsea House, 1995.

Bruchac, Joseph. *The Girl Who Married the Moon: Tales from Native North America*. Moraga, Calif.: Bridge Water Books, 1994.

Caduto, Michael J. *Keepers of the Night: Native American Stories and Nocturnal Activities for Children*. Boulder, Colo.: Fulcrum Press, 1994.

Freedman, Russell. *An Indian Winter*. New York: Holiday House, 1992.

Liptak, Karen. *North American Indian Survival Skills.* New York: Franklin Watts, 1990.

Monroe, Jean Guard. *First Houses: Native American Homes and Sacred Structures.* Boston: Houghton Mifflin, 1993.

Sattler, Helen Roney. *The Earliest Americans.* New York: Clarion Books, 1993.

White Deer of Autumn. *The Native American Book of Knowledge.* Hillsboro, Ore.: Beyond Woods, 1992.

Wolfson, Evelyn. *From Abenaki to Zuni: A Dictionary of Native American Tribes.* New York: Walker, 1988.

Wolfson, Evelyn. *From the Earth to Beyond the Sky: Native American Medicine.* Boston: Houghton Mifflin, 1993.

Young, Ed. *Moon Mother: A Native American Creation Tale.* New York: HarperCollins, 1993.

INDEX

Italicized page numbers indicate illustrations.

ABOUT THE AUTHOR

Popular author Elaine Landau worked as a newspaper reporter, an editor, and a youth services librarian before becoming a full-time writer. She has written more than ninety nonfiction books for young people, including *The Sioux, The Cherokees, The Hopi,* and *The Chilula*. Ms. Landau, who has a bachelor's degree in English and journalism from New York University and a master's degree in library and information science from Pratt Institute, lives in New Jersey with her husband and son.